Cooking Seafood

Comprehensive Beginners Guide on How to Make Mouthwatering Seafood Delicacies

Introduction

You are about to learn how to make mouthwatering seafood delicacies!

Do you love seafood?

Are you tired of dining out and ordering in?

Would you love to learn how to prepare delicious and mouthwatering seafood recipes?

If this is you, then you are in the right place; this book will cover a variety of seafood recipes you can prepare at home.

The thing about seafood is that if it is not well prepared, you are unlikely to enjoy it; however, if done well, you will love it. For most people, the challenge is how best to prepare delicious seafood.

If you want to learn how to prepare seafood and are wondering things like:

✓ How to choose quality fish and shellfish?

✓ How best to store your seafood to ensure it remains fresh longer?

✓ How best to prepare and cook seafood?

This book is for you.

This book will teach you:

- ✓ Ways to choose your next batch of seafood.

- ✓ **How to store fish and seafood properly**

- ✓ Methods of preparing various types of seafood.

- ✓ **Ten easy ways to cook seafood.**

- ✓ Mouthwatering shrimp and salmon recipes

- ✓ **Other fish and shellfish recipes**

- ✓ Mixed seafood recipes

- ✓ **And so much more!**

Even if you've never considered yourself a good cook, this book will turn you into a good seafood chef without trying too hard!

Let's get started:

PS: I'd like your feedback. If you are happy with this book, please leave a review on Amazon.

Please leave a review for this book on Amazon by visiting the page below:

https://amzn.to/2VMR5qr

Table of Content

Section 1: Why Eat Seafood?

"I cook with wine. Sometimes I even add it to the food."

– W.C. Fields

There is no question that seafood can improve your health. Years of scientific study have demonstrated that making seafood part of your diet can help you avoid many health problems, including depression, anemia, and other illnesses.

According to a 2020 analysis of 34 research results, those who consume more fish have decreased risks of depression, heart attacks, heart failure, coronary heart disease (CHD), strokes, and liver cancer.

Besides containing DHA and EPA, types of omega-3s that are great for your cognitive function and neurodevelopment, seafood has a lot of vitamins and minerals, including vitamin B12, zinc, and selenium. Fish and other seafood have all the required amino acids for optimal human health.

For example, a cooked 3-ounce fish or shellfish meal provides roughly one-third of your daily recommended amount of protein. According to studies,[1] incorporating

---

[1] https://pubmed.ncbi.nlm.nih.gov/27519920/

seafood dishes twice or thrice in your weekly meal schedule is an excellent way to meet your nutritional needs.

With that in mind, let's look at the best ways to choose nutritionally-safe fish and shellfish to incorporate into your meals:

Choosing Your Next Batch Of Seafood

When you shop for seafood, get fresh, well-harvested, and low-mercury fish and shellfish. When looking for fresh seafood, check out your neighborhood's established and specialized fish markets, local fishmongers, fishermen, and seafood counters.

Generally, when purchasing fish steaks or fillets, check that it meets the following conditions:

- The flesh is solid and not mushy.

- The fragrance is salty like the sea, not "fishy."

- There shouldn't be any evidence of freezer burn if you purchase it frozen.

When purchasing whole fish, choose only those that have the following characteristics:

- Shiny clean eyes and taut, brilliant skin with no missing scales.

- Bright and wet gills and firm, undamaged stomachs.

- Ask the fish dealer to "dress" the fish for you if you don't want to remove the scales, intestines, and gills.

How to Choose Fish With Low Mercury Levels

Seafood is a nutritious food that offers vital nutrients. However, while eating a lot of seafood may help prevent some diseases, how and what kind of seafood you eat is essential. For starters, there are significant levels of mercury in several types of seafood.

Consuming food with mercury has several adverse effects. Research[2] shows that in addition to weakening your immune system, excessive mercury levels may raise your risk of high blood pressure and heart attacks. Further, children exposed to excessive mercury levels in the womb may develop cognitive problems as adults.

---

[2] https://www.ncbi.nlm.nih.gov/pmc/articles/PMC3139210/

The most concerning dietary source of mercury in the world is **tuna**, particularly its commonly-served varieties. When you consume raw tuna frequently, it increases your risk of mercury buildup.[3]

You absorb mercury from it more easily than from cooked tuna. Other fish with **high mercury** content include **shark, swordfish, tilefish, and king mackerel.**

Fish and seafood with lower levels of mercury and POPs include the following:

- Salmon.

- Herring.

- Sardines.

- Haddock.

- Trout.

- Shellfish like oysters and clams, and cod.

---

[3] https://www.ncbi.nlm.nih.gov/pmc/articles/PMC5334723/

How to Choose Quality Shellfish

You want to purchase the freshest seafood available when shopping. To ensure you're obtaining the best quality, go by these recommendations.

1. While purchasing **crustaceans**, ensure they are **alive** and healthy.

2. While purchasing **shrimp**, the flesh should appear **juicy** and **bouncy**.

3. **Lobsters** should be **hefty** and plump, with all feet and **claws intact**.

4. Mollusks such as oysters, clams, and mussels should be alive or breathing at the time of purchase.

5. Keep an eye out for mollusks with securely shut shells. If a shell is partially open, touch it to check if it snaps back closed. If not, the mollusk is dead, and you should avoid it.

6. Shellfish need to smell like the ocean. Avoid any bad-smelling fish.

How to Store Fish Properly

You should cook fresh fish within 24 hours as the fish's texture and taste may deteriorate fast. If you want to refrigerate your fish or shellfish to chill before cooking, put it in a zipped bag on top of a basin of ice. Place all seafood in the refrigerator's coldest area, and ensure you throw it away when it starts smelling "fishy."

If you must freeze it, storing it in a container with ice beneath will keep it fresher longer than in a freezer bag. After two to three months, most fish will lose flavor and texture in the freezer.

Shellfish Preservation and Storage

You should boil and prepare your seafood quickly because shellfish spoil rapidly. Use these suggestions for shellfish storage, but remember that these tips will only keep your seafood fresh for a maximum of three days.

- Place live crustaceans on a bed of seaweed or moist newspaper in the refrigerator.

- Place oysters and clams on an ice layer with a paper towel covering them to prevent drying out, whereas you should completely submerge mussels in ice. Put the ice and mollusks in the refrigerator in a dish that can drain water.

- You can preserve shelled shrimp and scallops in plastic.

- You can refrigerate cephalopods like squid and octopus after washing them in water, putting them on a plate, and firmly wrapping them in plastic wrap.

With the basics covered, let's dive right into preparing seafood:

Section 2: Preparing Seafood

Here are the various key things you need to know about preparing seafood:

Fish Skinning & Bone Removal

Most of your purchased fish varieties will come de-boned and filleted. If that is not the case, you can get the bones out with tweezers or needle-nose pliers. While it may be challenging to find pin bones, you can quickly locate them by lightly rubbing your fingers over the meat and feeling for the bones—do so gently to avoid pricking your finger.

You can prepare some fish with the skin on, such as the sole or flounder. If you keep the skin, make hash marks on it with a knife. But if you need to peel the fish, lay it skin-side down on a chopping board.

Then, insert a chef's knife through the flesh and skin on the tail side of the fish's body. With the knife slightly slanted down, carefully cut the fillet. When you move the blade, hold the skin until its release. After that, use paper towels to pat the skin dry. Baking the skin will help it get pleasantly crispy.

While selecting a cooking technique, consider the type of fish. Your recipes are to your taste, but it's also vital to consider how the fish's inherent taste, thickness, and fat content will interplay with the cooking. For instance, you can panfry sole as it is lean, firm, and has a tasty skin, but it is unwise to panfry tuna since it is fatty and meaty.

Shellfish Preparation for Cooking

Crustaceans, including crab and lobster, often only require washing before cooking.

1. Discard the shrimp's shell and vein by manually locating the black vein in the center of the shrimp and tugging it out, or you can use a deveiner. Rinse to get rid of any leftovers.

2. Soak mollusks for approximately 20 minutes to get rid of sand. After cleaning them, pull the mollusk's beard back toward the hinge to remove it.

3. Typically, cephalopods need tenderizing before being cooked. You can do this by gently pounding, scoring the flesh, or marinating it in milk

Cleaning Clams and Mussels

Please ensure the clams and mussels you purchase are fresh since their health begins to decline once they are out of the water. Please keep them in your fridge or on ice before cooking.

Put the shellfish in a basin of ice water and let them soak for 20 minutes before you begin cooking. They will be able to "breathe" as a result, forcing out any sand trapped between their shells.

Scrub each mussel or clam under a stream of water after soaking. If any of your mussels have beards protruding from their shells, now is the time to remove them.

Give the beard a firm tug toward the mussel's hinge end. The mussel might be torn apart and killed if you pull the beard in the direction of the aperture. If the mussels and clams are still alive, they are ready to cook.

Different Ways to Cook Seafood

A description of each cooking technique is below, along with suggestions for fish.

1. Grilling fish fillets

Use this cooking method with heartier-textured seafood like salmon, swordfish, and tuna. Be on the lookout for thick steak slices, which are excellent for grilling.

To grill the fillets, set up a grill rack over medium-high heat, then oil the fish and sprinkle pepper and salt over it. Put the fillet on the grill, skin side down, and grill the fish for approximately 8 to 10 minutes for each inch of thickness. Thus, if the salmon fillet is an inch thick, grill it skin-side down for around 4-5 minutes before flipping it to finish. If the fillet is not too thick, you can enclose the grill and don't bother flipping it at all.

2. Cooking whole fish

Try this with trout, sea bass, or red snapper.

Add herbs, lemons, pepper, salt, and pepper to the fish cavity. Apply butter or olive oil to the fish's outside and grill it for 12 to 15 minutes, turning it once or until it is somewhat browned and cooked well.

3. Sautéing or pan-frying

Try this with salmon, halibut, sole, flounder, or other fish. These species have delicious, delicate skin. Skip sautéing tuna and swordfish.

Preheating the pan is necessary, whether you flour your fish lightly or leave it unadorned. For the pan to get hot enough, leave it on high heat for at least three minutes. After that, add a thin layer of cooking oil.

As the oil begins to smoke, season the fish fillets, then carefully set them in the pan, skin side down. If the fish is thin, you may maintain the heat on high. Lower it to medium if they are thick. After that, let it be. Fish will stick to the pan if you keep flipping it, which is terrible for a crisp crust.

Give the fish three minutes to fry. Turning it over to complete the other side will create a crust and release effortlessly, taking approximately a minute.

4. Deep-frying

Try this with Alaska cod, tilapia, halibut, Alaska pollock, or Louisiana catfish.

Dredge skinless fillets in flour, then in whisked eggs, and last in breadcrumbs or cornmeal. Brown for about 4 minutes in oil heated to 375°F.

5. Baking

Try this with Denser fish slices like halibut, sablefish, and Arctic char.

Drizzle fillets with melted butter and then season with your preferred herbs. Then bake the fish fillets in the oven for 40 to 50 minutes at 250°F. You will get delicate, juicy fillets with this low-and-slow technique.

6. Broiling

Any fish will work well, except for more than 3 pounds of huge fish, which is ideal for roasting. Wild black cod or salmon are excellent for broiling.

Place the rack approximately 3 inches from the broiler and let it heat up for 10 minutes. Place the fish on a glass dish or baking sheet and broil for 5 minutes or until golden. The technique works particularly well with glazes because the high heat caramelizes the fish.

7. Roasting

Try it with red snapper, trout, or sea bass. This approach works best for a whole fish or huge fillets or steaks.

Place your fish in a roasting pan or on a baking sheet coated with non-stick spray, and then rub it with pepper and salt. Use kitchen twine to shut the cavity of a whole fish after stuffing it with herbs, tomatoes, or lemons.

To enhance the flavor and guarantee moistness, drizzle olive oil on top and add a tiny quantity of white wine or chicken stock to the pan (just enough to cover the bottom).

It should take 20 to 30 minutes to roast a fish at 400°F, depending on its size. Use a thermometer with an immediate read setting (140°F) to check the temperature.

8. Poaching

Try this with Fatty fish, such as salmon and trout, and lean fish, such as tilapia, halibut, haddock, cod, sole, or snapper.

Poaching the fish in a seasoned liquid maintains the moisture while adding flavor. To poach the fish, combine chicken stock or white wine with some water in a saucepan to make the poaching liquid. Then add spices and vegetables like carrots, lemons, and leeks with herbs like garlic cloves, parsley dill, whole peppercorns, and tarragon. Then include spices, vegetables like carrots, lemons, and leeks with seasonings like garlic cloves, parsley dill, whole peppercorns, and tarragon. You should have enough liquid to cover your fish completely.

To slightly decrease the liquid and bring out the flavors, bring the fish to a boil and let it simmer for about 20 minutes. After that, carefully add the fish to the cooking liquid, then simmer for 6 to 10 minutes or until it flakes apart when tested with a fork. To remove the fish, use a slotted spoon.

Oven-poaching

Use this cooking method with delicate white fish, such as Pollack.

En papillote, or wrapping fish in separate small packets, is another way to poach fish with far less liquid. Place roughly 12 to 34 cups of chopped vegetables on a big piece of aluminum foil or parchment paper in each packet.

Place the fish on top of the veggies, then drizzle two tablespoons of chicken stock, white wine, or preferred marinade over the top. Fold the foil or parchment paper over the fish and crimp the edges tight. Bake the packets until an instant-read thermometer reads 140 degrees Fahrenheit in the center or 12 to 15 minutes at 400 degrees, depending on their thickness.

10. The pressure cooker method

Try this cooking method with scallops, salmon, cod, and lobsters.

Except for when you're making fish stews and chowders, slow cooking is only ideal for some seafood. Instead, it is better to use an Instant Pot for such recipes. If you want an alternative way to cook fish, try pressure cookers.

First, coat your fish in butter or frying oil, pepper, and salt to sear your skillet. Scallops, lobsters, salmon, and cod taste great when fried in a skillet.

As already noted, seafood preparation differs significantly from other forms of meat, so adopting such dishes for the first time might be scary. However, as you'll learn, inexperience is the main barrier to preparing quick and tasty seafood dishes. Cooking fish and seafood is easier when you comprehend the fundamentals of selecting and cooking seafood.

Lets now get to the specific mouthwatering seafood delicacies you can easily prepare at home:

Section 3: Mouthwatering Seafood Recipes

"A recipe has no soul. You, as the cook, must bring soul to the recipe."

– Thomas Keller

Section 3i: Salmon Recipes

1: Grilled Salmon with Tomatoes & Basil

Prep Time: 25 minutes

Cook Time: 15 minutes

Total Time: 40 minutes

Serves 4-6

Ingredients

- ¼ teaspoon pepper, freshly ground

- 2 medium tomatoes, thinly sliced

- 1/3 cup + ¼ cup fresh basil sliced thinly and divided

- 1 whole wild salmon fillet

- 1 tablespoon extra-virgin olive oil

- 1 teaspoon kosher salt divided

- 2 cloves garlic, minced

Directions

Over medium heat, preheat the grill and then mash minced garlic and salt on a cutting board to obtain a paste.

Pour the paste into a small bowl and stir in oil. Prep the salmon and remove any pin bones.

Line the cooking pan with heavy-duty foil, then put the salmon on the foil, skin side down.

Now spread the garlic mixture on the fish and then sprinkle with about 1/3 cup of basil.

Overlap the tomato slices and sprinkle with pepper and ¼ teaspoon salt.

Put the fish onto a foil on a grill, and then grill it until it flakes easily or for about 10-12 minutes.

Slide the salmon onto a serving platter using two large spatulas.

To serve the fish, sprinkle with chopped basil.

This dish pairs well with rosé or light-bodied, low-tannin red.

2: Baked Salmon with Chimichurri Sauce

Serves 4

Prep Time: 5 minutes

Cook Time: 35 minutes

Total Time: 40 minutes

Ingredients

For the salmon

- Freshly ground black pepper

- Kosher salt

- 1 ½ pounds Fresh Atlantic Salmon Side

For the chimichurri

- ½ teaspoon oregano

- ¼ teaspoon kosher salt

- 1 tablespoon fresh lemon juice

- 1 tablespoon red wine vinegar

- ½ cup organic extra virgin olive oil

- 1 garlic clove

- 2 green onion tops

- 1 cup tightly packed fresh parsley leaves and tender stems

- 1 cup of fresh cilantro leaves and tender stems (tightly packed)

- Freshly ground Black Pepper

- ¼ teaspoon kosher salt

Directions

Preheat the oven to 450F and line your baking sheet with parchment paper.

Mix cumin, olive oil, salt, and pepper in a large bowl.

Sprinkle the salmon thoroughly with some pepper and salt and put it on a baking sheet lined with parchment paper.

Bake until the salmon is flaky and well-cooked, which should take around 10 minutes. Check your fish with a fork so as not to overcook it.

As the fish cooks, make your sauce.

Prep the onion, add them and the rest of the ingredients to a blender, and puree until you get a fully blended sauce.

Serve the salmon drizzled with the sauce.

This dish pairs incredibly with a bright and crisp Sauv Blanc.

3: Quick Instant Pot Salmon

Prep Time: 5 minutes

Cook Time: 5 minutes

Total Time: 10 minutes

Serves: 4

Ingredients

- ¼ teaspoon of freshly ground black pepper, ground

- ¼ teaspoon of salt

- 1 tablespoon of butter, unsalted

- 1 bunch of dill, fresh

- 4 equal-sized frozen fillets of salmon, 5 oz

- ¾ cup water

- 3 medium lemon

Directions

Put the water and juiced lemon in the bottom of the cooking pot, then add the steamer insert.

Put the frozen salmon fillets on the steamer rack and sprinkle the dill, then put a fresh lemon slice on each of the fillets.

Secure the lid and set the timer to about 5 minutes.

As soon as the timer beeps, release the steam carefully and open the lid.

Serve the fish with lemon, extra dill, and butter.

This dish pairs well with Sauv Blanc or with Chardonnay.

4: Walnut-Crusted Salmon

Serves 2

Prep Time: 25 minutes

Cook Time: 15 minutes

Total Time: 40 minutes

Ingredients

- 1 tablespoon olive oil

- 2 3 oz. salmon fillets

- ¼ teaspoon dill

- ½ tablespoon Dijon mustard

- 2 tablespoon maple syrup, sugar-free

- ½ cup walnuts

- Salt and pepper to taste

Directions

First, preheat the oven to 350F. Meanwhile, in a food processor, grind ½ cup of walnuts.

Add the spices, syrup, and mustard to the food processor and pulse until you have a paste-like consistency.

Pat dry the salmon fillets thoroughly. Heat a tablespoon of oil in a skillet or pan until hot.

Put the dried fillet skin side facing down in the pan. Allow the fillets to sear for 3 minutes without turning them.

Spread the walnut mixture on top of the salmon fillets as they sear. Then transfer into the preheated oven and bake the mixture for 8 minutes.

Serve the salmon on a bed of spinach sprinkled with smoked paprika.

This dish pairs well with Marsanne.

5: Pan-Seared Salmon and Roasted Sprouts

Serves:2

Prep Time: 15 minutes

Cook Time: 15 minutes

Total Time: 30 minutes

Ingredients

- 1 tablespoon MCT oil

- 1/8 teaspoon salt

- 2 (4 to 6-ounce) salmon fillets

- 1 tablespoon olive or coconut oil

- ½ teaspoon smoked sea salt

- ½ cup coarsely chopped walnuts

- 2 tablespoons olive oil

- Fresh cracked black pepper to taste

- 1 pound Brussels sprouts, halved

- Lemon wedges for serving

Directions

First, preheat the oven to 400F.

Drizzle about 2 tablespoons of oil, some smoked sea salt, and cracked black pepper on the Brussels sprouts, mix until coated, and put them and the walnuts in a roasting dish. Roast the mixture for approximately 20 minutes or until slightly browned.

Heat a tablespoon of coconut or olive oil over medium-high heat in an oven-safe pan.

Season the salmon fillets with smoked sea salt and cracked black pepper to taste. Cook until the salmon is golden, or for about 4 minutes per side.

Transfer the salmon to the preheated oven and cook for another 6 minutes.

You can serve individual salmon fillets with a three-quarter cup of roasted Brussels sprouts. Sprinkle half a tablespoon of MCT oil on each fillet, and enjoy!

This dish pairs well with a German Riesling

6: Salmon, Kale & Sweet Potatoes

Serves 2

Prep Time: 20 minutes

Cook Time: 30 minutes

Total Time: 50 minutes

Ingredients

- 12 cherry or grape tomatoes

- 1 pat butter

- 1½ teaspoons freshly ground black pepper,

- 1 ½ teaspoons kosher salt

- 3 tablespoons olive oil

- 1 lemon

- 1 grapefruit

- 1 orange

- 1 lb. filet of wild salmon

- 1 bunch kale

- 1 sweet potato

Directions

Allumette the sweet potatoes and then toss them with a tablespoon of olive oil, salt, and pepper to taste, orange zest, and a tablespoon of orange juice.

Prepare the kale and toss each with a tablespoon of grapefruit juice and olive oil, salt and pepper to taste, and grapefruit zest.

Coat the salmon with 2 tablespoons of lemon juice, virgin olive oil, salt and pepper to taste, and lemon zest. Cut the wild-caught salmon in half.

Now put each half of the fillet skin side down between the kale and potatoes in your two dishes.

Top each dish with a lemon slice and a pat of butter. Then put three grape or cherry tomatoes on the sides of each salmon fillet.

Bake this in the oven at 400F for approximately 25 minutes.

This dish pairs well with a full-bodied white wine such as a Viognier.

7: Almond Salmon with Roasted Fennel

Serves 2

Prep Time: 20 minutes

Cook Time: 1 hour 20 minutes

Total Time: 1 hour 40 minutes

Ingredients

- 2 tablespoons shaved almonds

- 2 teaspoons pure local honey, organic

- 2 8-oz wild salmon fillets

- Lemon juice

- Smoked sea salt

- Olive oil

- 1 fennel bulb

- Roasted Fennel

Directions

Preheat your oven to around 400F.

Cut the fennel stems, which you can preserve for garnish or soups if desired. Then chop the white bulb into chunks and drizzle with olive oil, pepper, and smoked sea salt.

While uncovered, roast the fennel for around 30 minutes.

Spread honey on salmon fillets and top with shaved almonds. Sprinkle a small pinch of the smoked sea salt on the shaved almonds.

Place the salmon on a roasting pan with the skin side facing down. After the fennel has been in the oven for 30 minutes, add the salmon.

Bake both for 12 minutes or until the fish cooks and the almonds brown.

This dish pairs well with Pinot Noir.

8: Prosciutto-wrapped Salmon Skewers

Serves 4

Prep Time: 50 minutes

Cook Time: 30 minutes

Total Time: 1 hour 20 minutes

Ingredients

- 1 tablespoon olive oil

- 3 oz. prosciutto, in slices

- 1 pinch of freshly ground black pepper

- 1 lb. salmon, semi-thawed

- ¼ cup fresh basil, finely chopped

- ½ cup mayonnaise

Directions

First, soak the skewers in water for approximately 30 minutes. Meanwhile, finely chop the basil using a sharp knife.

Now cut the semi-thawed salmon lengthwise and skewer them lengthwise.

Roll the fillet-mounted skewers in the chopped basil and pepper.

Thinly slice the prosciutto, wrap the meat around the fish, then coat with olive oil.

Fry the skewers in a pan, grill, or cook in the oven until cooked.

Serve with a fresh salad and aioli on the side.

This dish pairs well with Semillon.

9: Stuffed Salmon Rolls with Lemon Sauce

Prep Time:15 minutes

Cook Time:15 minutes

Total Time:30 minutes

Serves: 4

Ingredients

- 2 teaspoons cornstarch

- 2 tablespoons lemon juice

- 1/2 cup chicken broth

- 1 tablespoon butter

- ½-pound asparagus, trimmed

- Salt and pepper to taste

- 2 teaspoons of lemon zest

- 2 tablespoons basil, chopped

- ½ cup Parmesan cheese, grated

- 1 (12-ounce) container of ricotta

- 4 (5-ounce) salmon fillets, skins removed

Directions

Season the salmon with pepper and salt, then lay them with the skin side facing up.

Top the salmon fillets with lemon zest, basil, Parmesan, ricotta, salt, and pepper. Add a few spears of asparagus and roll the salmon.

Put the mixture on a greased baking sheet with the seam side facing down.

Bake in a preheated oven at 425F for 15 to 20 minutes or until the salmon cooks.

Over medium heat, melt some butter in a saucepan and add the mixture of cornstarch, lemon juice, and broth.

Cook for 3 to 5 minutes or until the mixture thickens.

Serve the rolls topped with lemon sauce and garnish with lemon zest and basil.

This dish pairs well with Chardonnay or Sauvignon Blanc.

10: Salmon and Quinoa Bowls with Yogurt Sauce

Serves 4

Prep Time 15 minutes

Cook Time 15 minutes

Total Time 30 minutes

Ingredients

- 2 tablespoons dried currants, cranberries, or cherries

- 2 cups cooked chickpeas, rinsed and drained

- Sea salt

- Olive oil

- 2 garlic cloves, minced

- 2 tablespoons lemon juice

- 1 medium carrot, peeled and thinly sliced

- 1 bunch of dinosaur kale, thinly sliced

- 1 cup white quinoa

- Four 4-ounce sockeye salmon fillets

- 1 tablespoon hemp seeds

For the sauce:

- ½ teaspoon sea salt

- ½ cup Greek yogurt

- 1 tablespoon lemon juice

- ½ cup water

- ¼ cup tahini paste

Directions

Mix 2 cups of water and quinoa in a medium saucepan.

Bring to a boil, cover, and keep the heat low. Cook for around 15 minutes, then set aside for 10 minutes.

Mix sea salt, 2 tablespoons of olive oil, garlic, lemon juice, carrots, and kale in a large mixing bowl.

Toss the kale with your hands until well coated in oil and lemon. Add the cooked quinoa, hemp seeds, dried fruits, and chickpeas. Mix well, adjusting the seasoning as desired.

In a cast iron skillet or non-stick skillet, heat 2 tablespoons of oil. Pat the fish dry and season with some salt.

Cook the fish over high heat, skin-side down, for about 2-3 minutes or until nicely browned. Flip the salmon and cook until it is opaque up the sides, in 2 minutes.

In a mixing bowl, add the ¼ cup tahini, 1 tablespoon lemon juice, ½ cup Greek yogurt, and ½ teaspoon sea salt and mix until a smooth mixture forms. Add the water gradually to the smooth mixture to achieve your preferred consistency.

Divide the quinoa between serving plates and top with seared fish. Spoon the sauce over the salmon and serve.

Section 3ii: Shrimp Recipes

11: Garlic Lemon Chive Grilled Shrimp

Serves 4

Prep Time: 30 minutes

Cook Time: 10 minutes

Total Time: 40 minutes

Ingredients

- 1 loaf of crusty French bread for dipping

- 1 lemon

- 3 cloves fresh garlic, chopped

- ¼ cup fresh chives, chopped

- ½ stick of softened butter

- 1 pound shrimp, with shells but deveined

Directions

Start by preparing the herb butter. Mix the chives, garlic, softened butter, and zest from half a lemon and stir to blend.

Cut two big pieces of foil and lay them on each other to ensure none of the butter sauce runs out.

Pick the shrimp and arrange half of the raw shrimp at the center of the two pieces of aluminum foil.

Pick half of the butter mixture, put it on top of the fish, then roll the center of the foil and move on all sides until you create a secure foil pouch.

Repeat all the steps for the other half of the shrimp that you have two pouches.

Put the shrimp on a preheated grill and cook for about 8 minutes. Do not cook for any longer because it may overcook.

Serve the shrimp with crusty French bread, fresh lemon slices, and chives.

12: Crock-pot Shrimp Fra Diavolo

Prep Time: 15 minutes

Cook Time: 2 hours 25 minutes

Total Time: 2 hours 40 minutes

Serves 4

Ingredients

- ¼ pound of medium-sized shelled shrimp

- ½ teaspoon black pepper, freshly ground

- 1 tablespoon Italian parsley, minced

- 1 (14.5-ounce) can of fire-roasted tomatoes, diced

- 1 teaspoon red pepper flakes

- 3-5 cloves of garlic, minced

- 1 medium onion, diced

- 1 teaspoon avocado or olive oil

Directions

In a non-stick frying pan, heat some oil over medium heat.

Sauté garlic, onion, and pepper flakes until the onion has softened and is translucent, which should take 8 to 10 minutes.

Add black pepper, parsley, tomatoes, and the onion mixture to a slow cooker. Stir to blend, then cook for 2 to 3 hours on low heat.

Add in shrimp, then stir and cover. Cook until cooked through or for 15 minutes on high heat. Serve and enjoy.

13: Spicy Garlic Shrimp

Serves 4

Prep Time: 15 minutes

Cook Time: 15 minutes

Total Time: 30 minutes

Ingredients

- ¼ cup freshly parsley, chopped

- ¼ cup chicken broth, fat-free

- ¼ cup dry white wine

- 2 dozen jumbo raw shrimp, peeled, deveined

- ½ teaspoon red pepper flakes

- 4 cloves garlic, peeled and crushed

- 2 tablespoons olive oil

- Pepper, fresh ground

- Salt

Directions

In a skillet, heat oil over medium-high heat. Add shrimp and cook it until no longer pink in color; this should take about 4 to 5 minutes.

Remove the shrimp from the heat and let it cool. Add red pepper flakes and garlic to the skillet and sauté for a minute.

Remove the skillet from the heat, set aside the shrimp, and add wine to deglaze it. Return the pan to heat, add in broth, and allow to thicken.

Once thickened to your preferred consistency, add in parsley. At this point, return the shrimp to the skillet and toss it to coat.

Remove from the burner and serve it over preferred whole grains such as brown rice or quinoa.

14: Grilled Rosemary Garlic Shrimp

Total: 18 minutes

Prep: 10 minutes

Cook: 8 minutes

Serves 4

Ingredients

- 16 jumbo shrimp

- 3 tablespoons olive oil plus oil for brushing shrimp

- 2 tablespoons minced fresh rosemary leaves

- 1 teaspoon sea salt

- ¼ cup finely chopped garlic

- Rosemary sprigs for garnish

- Lemon wedges

Directions

First, mash salt and garlic in a bowl; add olive oil, minced rosemary, and shrimp, and mix to coat evenly.

Let the shrimp marinate in the fridge for 1 to 2 hours. Meanwhile, preheat the grill.

After 1-2 hours, remove the shrimp from the refrigerator, and put about 4 shrimp on an individual pre-soaked skewer. Brush the shrimp with oil.

Grill until cooked through or for about 3 or 4 minutes per side.

15: Shrimp-Avocado Salad

Serves 8

Prep Time: 20 minutes

Cook Time: 20 minutes

Total Time: 40 minutes

Ingredients

- ½ bunch of cilantro, washed

- 2 tablespoons lime juice, freshly squeezed

- 1 jalapeño chilies, seedless and finely diced

- 4 garlic cloves, minced

- 1 medium onion, finely diced

- 2 avocados, peeled and cut into chunks

- 1 lb. assorted fresh cherry tomatoes, sliced

- 1½ pound shrimp, peeled, deveined; cut into pieces

- Salt and fresh cracked pepper to taste

Directions

Start by boiling a pot of salted water and then add shrimp to the boiling water. Meanwhile, prepare a bowl of ice-cold water.

Simmer until it turns pink and almost cooks through.

Remove the shrimp from the salty water, place them in the ice water, and let them cool completely.

Add the seasoning to the remaining ingredients in a large bowl.

Add salt and pepper or more jalapenos and lime if needed. Serve the salad in avocado shells, bowls, or glasses.

16: Grilled Blackened Shrimp Tacos

Preparation: 15 minutes

Cooking: 5 minutes

Ready-In: 20 minutes

Serves 4

Ingredients

- ½ cup prepared pico de gallo

- ½ cup fresh cilantro leaves

- 2 cups iceberg lettuce, chopped

- 8 corn tortillas, warmed

- 2 tablespoons salt-free Cajun spice blend

- 1 pound large raw shrimp, peeled and deveined

- ¼ teaspoon salt

- 1 small garlic clove, grated

- 1 tablespoon lime juice

- 1 ripe avocado

Directions

Heat the grill to medium to high.

In a bowl, mash avocado well and add salt, garlic, and lemon juice. Stir well.

Pat dry the fish, then toss it in a medium bowl with the seasoning.

Thread the seasoned fish on metal skewers and grill, turning once for about 4 minutes or until cooked.

Serve the fish in tortillas, topped with pico de gallo, cilantro, lettuce, and guacamole.

17: Shrimp & Sausage Skillet Dinner

Prep Time: 5 minutes

Cook time: 15 minutes

Total Time: 20 minutes

Servings: 4

Ingredients

- 1 medium red pepper cut into 2-inch slices

- ½ lb. green beans cut into 2-inch pieces

- 1 clove garlic minced

- 1 jalapeno minced

- 12 ounces chicken sausage cut into 1/2-inch slices

- 1 teaspoon Old Bay seasoning or Cajun Seasoning

- 1 pound shrimp peeled and deveined

- ¼ cup avocado oil divided

- Salt and pepper

Directions

Add 2 tablespoons of avocado oil to a large skillet and heat over medium-high.

Once it starts to shimmer, add shrimp in a single layer. Cook for around 2 minutes, flip, and season well.

Cook the shrimp until it's pink, then move it to a plate.

Heat the remaining avocado oil in the pan until shimmering. Add the sausage and cook for 2 or 3 minutes or until it starts browning.

Add garlic and jalapeno, and sauté the mixture for about 30 seconds or until fragrant.

Add the veggies and cook for 5 to 10 minutes more or until tender. Season everything with salt and pepper to taste.

Return the shrimp to the pan and warm it for two minutes. Serve.

18: Asian Shrimp Stir-Fry with Buckwheat Noodles

Serves 1

Ingredients

- 100ml or ½ cup chicken stock

- 50g kale or ¾ cup, roughly chopped

- 75g or ½ cup green beans, chopped

- 45g or ½ cup celery, trimmed and sliced

- 20g or ⅛ cup red onions, sliced

- 1 teaspoon fresh ginger, finely chopped

- 1 bird's eye chili, finely chopped

- 2 garlic cloves, finely chopped

- 75g or 3 ounces buckwheat noodles

- 2 teaspoons extra virgin olive oil

- 2 teaspoons tamari or soy sauce

- 150g or 1/3 pound shelled raw jumbo shrimp, deveined

Directions

Preheat a frying pan over a high heat setting. Once hot enough, cook the prawns in a teaspoon of oil and tamari for approximately 2 to 3 minutes.

Move the prawns to a plate, use kitchen paper to wipe and clean the pan, and set aside.

Now cook the noodles in boiling water based on the package directions or for approximately 5 to 8 minutes. Drain the noodles and set them aside.

Fry the red onion, chili, garlic, kale, beans, and celery in the reserved oil for 2 to 3 minutes over medium-high heat.

Add the chicken stock, bring the mixture to a boil, then simmer until the veggies are well cooked but crunchy, or for 1 to 2 minutes.

Add the celery leaves, noodles, and prawns to the pan and bring the mixture to a boil.

Finally, remove from the heat and enjoy.

19: Sesame Shrimp Stir Fry with Veggies

Prep time: 10 minutes

Cook time: 10 minutes

Total time: 20 minutes

Serves 4

Ingredients

- 2 cups rainbow chard, thinly sliced

- 2 garlic cloves minced

- 3 ounces shitake mushrooms, thinly sliced

- 1 small yellow squash cut into matchsticks

- 1 bell pepper seeded and sliced

- 1 small yellow onion, halved and thinly sliced

- 1 pound large wild shrimp, peeled and deveined

- 2 tablespoons coconut oil, divided

- 2 tablespoons shelled hemp seed, organic

- 2 tablespoons raw honey

- 2 teaspoons sesame oil

- ¼ cup liquid aminos or soy sauce

Directions

Mix hemp seeds, raw honey, sesame oil, and liquid aminos in a mixing bowl.

Heat a tablespoon of coconut oil in a large non-stick skillet or wok. Add shrimp and stir-fry for 2 minutes on high heat. Move it to a bowl and set it aside when it's no longer pink.

Add the remaining oil and stir-fry the shitakes, squash, peppers, and onion for 5 minutes, until lightly charred.

Add garlic and cook for a minute or until fragrant. Stir in chard and cook for about 2 minutes or until wilted.

Add the sauce and simmer for 2 more minutes until it thickens slightly. Finally, fold in the shrimp and cook for a minute.

Serve the fish and veggies over quinoa or brown rice.

20: Garlic Lemon Chive Grilled Shrimp

Prep time: 15 minutes

Cook time: 8 minutes

Total time: 13 minutes

Serves 4-6

Ingredients

- 1 loaf of crusty French bread, for dipping

- 1 lemon

- 3 cloves fresh garlic, chopped

- ¼ cup fresh chives, chopped

- ½ stick of softened butter

- 1 pound shrimp, with shells but deveined

Directions

Start by preparing the herb butter. Mix the chives, garlic, and softened butter. Add in the zest of half a lemon and stir to blend.

Now cut two large enough pieces of foil and lay them on each other to ensure none of the butter sauce pours out.

Pick the shrimp and arrange half of the raw shrimp at the center of the middle of pieces of aluminum foil.

Pick half of the butter mixture and put it on the fish. Now, roll the center of the foil and roll on all sides until you create a secure foil pouch.

Repeat all the steps for the other half of the shellfish to have two pouches if you use one pound of shrimp.

Place the shrimp on a preheated grill and cook for about 8 minutes. Do not cook for any longer so as not to overcook.

Serve the shrimp with crusty French bread, fresh lemon slices, and a sprinkling of chives.

Section 3iii: Other Fish Recipes

We shall focus on the recipes for tuna, halibut, trout, whitefish, bass, and catfish

21: Seared Tuna Steak

Prep Time: 15 minutes

Cook Time: 6 minutes

Total Time: 21 minutes

Serves 2

Ingredients

- 1 teaspoon sesame seeds

- 1 tablespoon sesame oil

- 2 tablespoons soy sauce

- 2 (6-ounce) ahi tuna steaks

- Salt and pepper

Directions

Sprinkle salt and pepper on your tuna steaks and place them in a shallow bowl.

Whisk together sesame oil and soy sauce and pour over the seasoned tuna steaks. Turn to evenly coat, then let marinate for approximately 15 minutes.

Over medium-high heat, heat a large skillet until it's very hot.

Add the steaks and cook until cooked or for 3 minutes. Flip and let the tuna cook for another 2 or 3 minutes.

Slice the tuna into half-inch slices and serve garnished with sesame seeds.

22: Grilled Halibut with Tomatoes and Hearts of Palm

Preparation: 15 minutes

Cooking: 5 minutes

Ready-In: 20 minutes

Serves 4-6

Ingredients

- ½ cup of hearts of palm (sliced and drained)

- 2 pounds mixed heirloom tomatoes, sliced

- Kosher salt

- Pepper, freshly ground

- 1 lemon

- Four 5–6-ounce halibut fillets (skinless and boneless)

- ¼ cup olive oil, plus more for grill and drizzling

- Torn basil leaves

Directions

Preheat the grill to medium heat and coat the grates well with oil.

Add 1 teaspoon of lemon zest, salt, and pepper to taste and some olive oil to the fish. Grill the fish, turning once, for around 5 minutes or until opaque in the middle and browned on both sides.

Mix ¼ cup olive oil, hearts of palm, and tomatoes in a bowl as the halibut cooks.

Add 2 tablespoons of lemon juice, salt, pepper, and basil and toss well.

Serve the fish topped with tomatoes and the dressing.

23: Mesquite Garlic Trout

Prep Time: 25 minutes

Cook Time: 25 minutes

Total Time: 50 minutes

Serves 4

Ingredients

- 4 tablespoons of minced garlic

- 1 teaspoon salt

- 1 teaspoon mesquite seasoning

- 2 pounds trout

Directions

First, preheat your outside grill or oven to 450F. Cut the tail and head of the well-cleaned fish.

Put 4 to 5 tablespoons of minced garlic in the open belly of the fish.

Pour some salt and mesquite seasoning on the garlic, then wait for the trout belly to close naturally.

Place the fish on an aluminum foil and loosely wrap it on the fish to fully seal it but with some air spaces.

Put the trout on the grill or oven and cook for about 20 minutes. As soon as the meat can easily flake, stop cooking and serve.

24: Broiled Tilapia Parmesan

Prep Time: 5 minutes

Cook Time: 10 minutes

Total Time: 15 minutes

Serves 8

Ingredients

- 2 pounds tilapia fillets

- 1/8 teaspoon smoked sea salt

- 1/8 teaspoon onion powder

- ¼ teaspoon black pepper, ground

- ¼ teaspoon dried basil

- 2 tablespoons fresh lemon juice

- 3 tablespoons mayonnaise

- ¼ cup of softened butter

- ½ cup Parmesan cheese

Directions

Preheat the broiler in the oven. As the oven preheats, coat a broiling pan with oil or line it with aluminum foil.

Mix lemon juice, mayonnaise, butter, and Parmesan cheese in a small bowl.

Season the mixture with smoked sea salt, onion powder, pepper, and dried basil and mix well.

Layer the fillets on the greased pan and broil for 2-3 minutes. Flip the fish and broil the other side for a few minutes.

Once ready, remove the fish from the oven and cover it with the cheese mixture.

Broil for another 2 minutes or until the fillets flake with a fork and the cheese has browned.

Serve and enjoy!

25: Pesto Catfish Packets

Serves 8

Prep Time: 20 minutes

Cook Time: 10 minutes

Total Time: 30 minutes

Ingredients

- Lime slices

- 1 pint of cherry tomatoes cut into halves

- Black pepper, freshly ground

- 1 1/2 teaspoons salt

- 1/2 cup jarred pesto

- 8 (6-ounce) catfish fillets

- 1/4 cup extra-virgin olive oil

Directions

Preheat the grill over medium-high heat. Then cut 8 pieces of foil, measuring approximately 8 by 11 inches.

Drizzle oil over each piece of foil and put the catfish fillets on top of the oil. Spread about 1 tablespoon of pesto over each fish fillet.

Season with salt and pepper, then top with lime slices and tomatoes.

Seal the packets and put them on the preheated grill's rack. Cook until the fish is opaque or for about 10 minutes.

26: Crispy Baked Fish Sticks

Prep Time: 10 minutes

Cook Time: 15 minutes

Total Time: 25 minutes

Serves 4

Ingredients

- 1 teaspoon water

- 1 large egg

- 1 (3.5-ounce) bag of pork rinds

- 1 1/2 tablespoons coconut flour

- 12 ounces fresh cod fillets

Directions

Preheat your oven to 400F. Meanwhile, cut the cod fillets into strips and season them with salt and pepper.

Sprinkle the cod fillets with coconut flour, then toss. Put the pork rinds in a Ziplock freezer bag and crush them into crumbs.

Once done, whisk the egg and water together and then dip each cod stick into the egg mixture.

Dredge the cod sticks in the pork crumbs and put them on a prepared baking sheet.

Bake until golden brown or for 12 to 15 minutes. Serve and enjoy.

27: Cod with Olives and Lemon

Serves 4

Prep Time: 30 minutes

Cook Time: 10 minutes

Total Time: 40 minutes

Ingredients

- 1 teaspoon lemon peel

- 24 oz boneless cod

- 20 each pitted kalamata olives

- 1 fl oz lemon juice

- 4 tablespoon butter stick, unsalted

- 1 teaspoon lemon zest

- 1 tablespoon avocado oil

- 8 cups broccoli florets

Directions

Add the juice of a lemon, diced olives, and butter to a bowl and combine using a fork.

Add salt, pepper, lemon zest, and 2 tablespoons of lemon juice and mix.

Add oil to a skillet and sauté broccoli over medium-high heat for 5-6 minutes or until softened.

Season the cod with salt and pepper. Broil or grill on each side for 3-4 minutes until it is white and firm.

Plate with broccoli, and top with a quarter of the olive butter.

28: Baked Whitefish with Tomatoes & Olives

Serves 2

Prep Time: 15 minutes

Cook Time: 25 minutes

Total Time: 40 minutes

Ingredients

- ¼ cup black or kalamata olives, pitted

- 1 tablespoon white wine

- 1 pint of cherry or grape tomatoes, halved

- 1 tablespoon extra-virgin olive oil

- 2 garlic cloves, crushed

- 2 4-5-ounce whitefish fillets de-skin and de-boned

- Your favorite seasoning blend

- A handful of fresh basil, finely chopped

Directions

Preheat the oven to 425 F.

Add the oil into an oven--safe skillet and heat over medium heat. As soon as the oil begins to shimmer, add in the garlic.

Cook the garlic until it's fragrant—not browned—or for about 1 minute while stirring.

Add tomatoes to the skillet with garlic and stir in the wine. Then remove the skillet from heat.

Season the fish fillets and put them in a pan, ensuring they touch the bottom.

Top the fillets with basil leaves and olives. Then spoon the pan juice and tomatoes onto the fillets.

Move the skillet to the oven and cook the mixture for 10 to 15 minutes or until the fish cooks.

Serve the whitefish and tomatoes olive dish topped with summer squash and zucchini.

29: 4 Ingredient Mahi Mahi

Servings 4

Prep Time: 5 minutes

Cook Time: 20 minutes

Total Time: 30 minutes

Ingredients

- 1 teaspoon salt

- 1 tablespoon Herbes de Provence

- ½ cup melted butter

- 4 Mahi Mahi fillets

Directions

First, preheat your oven to 375 degrees F. Meanwhile, put the Mahi Mahi fillets in a 9 by 13-inch pan.

Pour melted butter over the fillets and season with salt and Herbes de Provence.

Bake in the oven for about 20 minutes, then remove from heat. Let cool for 5 minutes and serve.

30: Low-Carb Pesto Baked Sea Bass

Prep Time: 5 minutes

Cook Time: 10 minutes

Total Time: 15 minutes

Serves 2

Ingredients

4 tablespoons pesto

1 tablespoon fresh lemon juice

1 tablespoon ghee, butter, or coconut oil

2 large sea bass fillets

Salt to taste

Directions

Preheat the oven to 400F. Put the sea bass with the skin facing down into a baking dish lined with baking paper.

Season the sea bass with salt and brush the tops using ghee. Then add in a squeeze of lemon and put in the oven.

Bake for about 10 minutes or until cooked through. Remove from the oven and top each serving with pesto.

Return the dish to the oven and bake for 3 to 5 minutes.

Remove from heat and allow to cool for around 5 minutes. Serve it hot, topped with preferred veggies and garlic.

Section 3 iv: Shellfish Recipes

This section will focus on recipes for the following seafood: crab, lobster, octopus, oysters, clams, mussels, prawns, and scallops.

31: Herb Lobster Tails on the Grill

- Preparation: 10 minutes

- Cooking: 12 minutes

- Ready-In: 22 minutes

- Serves 4

Ingredients

- ½ teaspoon black pepper

- ½ teaspoon red pepper flakes

- ½ teaspoon chili powder

- 1 teaspoon salt

- 1 teaspoon honey

- 1 tablespoon white wine

- 1 tablespoon fresh thyme

- 2 cloves garlic, minced

- 2 large sage leaves

- 4-5 large basil leaves

- ¼ cup fresh oregano leaves

- Juice of 1 lemon

- ¼ cup olive oil

- 4 large lobster tails, cut in half lengthwise

Directions

Mix all the ingredients in a food processor, skipping the lobster, to make herb topping. Add extra honey if need be.

Heat your grill to medium heat. Meanwhile, cut the lobster tails lengthwise using kitchen shears.

Rinse with water and pat dry. Put the tails onto a grill, the shell side sitting directly on the grill.

Now spoon the herb mixture onto the fleshy part of the fish and cover the grill.

Cook until cooked through or for about 8 to 12 minutes. Serve and enjoy!

32: Chipotle Grilled Mussels

Serves 8

Ingredients

- 2 fl oz sauvignon Blanc wine

- 2 pounds blue mussels

- 1 plum red tomato

- 2 tablespoons cilantro

- 2 chipotle en adobo

- 2 large scallions or spring onions

- 6 tablespoon unsalted butter stick

Directions

Heat a grill to medium heat. Then add tomato, cilantro, chipotles, scallions, and butter to a heavy-duty foil cooking bag.

Add in wine and mussels, and tightly close the bag. Please put it on a sheet pan in the fit ridge until the grill is ready.

Gently slide the bag onto the grill and cook for 10 to 12 minutes or until the bag puffs up.

Remove the bag from the grill using oven mitts and place it onto the sheet pan.

Unseal the bag to ensure the mussels have opened; otherwise, reseal and cook for another 3 to 5 minutes.

Finally, remove from the grill, cut open the bag, and pull back the foil. Spoon the juice in the bag over the mussels and serve.

33: Scallop and Cherry Tomato Skewers

Preparation: 13 minutes

Cooking: 12 minutes

Ready-In: 25 minutes

Serves 4

Ingredients

- 16 large sea scallops

- 24 cherry tomatoes

- 1 teaspoon salt

- 2 tablespoons Dijon mustard

- 2 tablespoons olive oil

- 1 lemon

- 8 (8-inch) bamboo skewers

Directions

Soak the skewers in hot water for over 30 minutes. Then preheat the grill for direct grilling to medium heat.

Whisk together 1½ teaspoons of grated lemon peel, 1 tablespoon of lemon juice, Dijon, and 1/8 teaspoon salt until blended.

Alternate between 2 scallops and 3 tomatoes on each skewer, beginning and ending with tomato.

Coat the tomatoes and fish with half of the Dijon and lemon mixture and place on the preheated grill grate.

Cook, occasionally turning for 7 to 9 minutes. Brush with the remaining lemon mixture and cook until the fish is fully opaque or for another 5 minutes.

34: Grilled Oysters with Chorizo Butter

Preparation: 15 minutes

Cooking: 30 minutes

Ready-In: 45 minutes

Serves 8

Ingredients

- 18 Louisiana or any other medium to large oysters, scrubbed

- 2 tablespoons fresh lime juice

- 1-½ sticks of unsalted butter cut into ½-inch cubes

- 4 ounces fresh Mexican chorizo, casings removed

- Salt

- Lime zest, finely grated

- Cilantro leaves

Directions

First, cook the chorizo in a skillet over moderate heat for 8 minutes or until lightly browned, breaking it up with a spoon.

Then scrape the chorizo into a bowl and break it into clumps.

Add 1 tablespoon of water over low heat to the skillet.

Add butter cubes individually while whisking until each cube has melted.

Stir in the cooked chorizo and lime juice and season them with salt. Keep the mixture warm over low heat.

Meanwhile, light a grill and put the oysters on the grill, the flat side facing up.

Grill the shellfish until the shells open slightly, then move them to a platter. Remove the top shell from the oysters using mitts or gloves.

Once done, spoon the chorizo onto the shellfish and serve it garnished with lime zest and cilantro leaf.

35: Pressure-Cooker Octopus

Serves 6

Prep Time: 20 minutes

Cook Time: 40 minutes

Total Time: 1 hour

Ingredients

- 2 ½-pound whole octopus, rinsed well

- Sea salt

Directions

Put the octopus in the pressure cooker's cooking pot and add enough water to cover it.

Season with salt, seal the lid, and let the cooker reach high pressure at 12 to 15 psi. Then cook the octopus at high pressure for 15 minutes. Then, quick release to depressurize the pressure cooker.

Slide a paring knife into the thickest part of the tentacles to check if the octopus is tender. The blade should slide easily.

If the octopus isn't tender, cook for another 5 minutes. Allow the fish to cool inside the cooking liquid and then drain. You can choose the store the octopus in the fridge for up to 2 days.

To serve, cut out and discard the hard beak found in the center of the base of its body where its tentacles converge.

Cut out the section of the head with eyes and discard, and separate the tentacles into individual pieces. These and the other parts are edible.

Serve the octopus cold. Cut the head and tentacles into bitesize pieces, then add them to a salad or any meal and enjoy.

36: Low-Carb Crab Soup

Prep time: 15 Minutes

Cook time: 25 Minutes

Total time: 40 Minutes

Servings: 7 cups

Ingredients

- Dash of smoked paprika

- ½ cup of green onion, tops only, chopped

- 1 cup of freshly grated Parmesan cheese

- ½ teaspoon of hot sauce

- ½ teaspoon of white pepper

- ½ teaspoon of salt

- ½ teaspoon of mace

- ¼ cup of sherry

- 1 pound of white crab meat

- 1 cup of whole milk

- 2 cups of fish or seafood stock

- 3 tablespoons of all-purpose flour

- 1 ½ cups of celery, finely diced (like 3 large stalks)

- 1 cup of sweet or yellow onion, diced

- 4 tablespoons of unsalted butter

- 1 cup heavy whipping cream

Directions

Heat the butter in a big heavy-bottomed cooking pot over medium-high heat until it melts.

Sauté the celery and onion for approximately 10 minutes or until tender. Whisk in the all-purpose flour, then pour in the seafood stock, constantly whisking until the mixture is smooth.

Reduce the heat to medium, then gently add the heavy cream while whisking. Add in whole milk as well while whisking.

Mix in the spices, sherry, and white crab meat. Set the heat to medium-low and allow the soup to simmer.

Once the soup heats up, adjust the seasonings.

Serve the crab soup warm. You can garnish every bowl with paprika, oyster crackers, chopped green onion, and fresh Parmesan cheese.

37: Grilled Oysters with Chorizo Butter

Preparation: 15 minutes

Cooking: 30 minutes

Ready-In: 45 minutes

Serves 8

Ingredients

- 18 Louisiana or any other medium to large oysters, scrubbed

- 2 tablespoons fresh lime juice

- 1-½ sticks of unsalted butter, cut into 1/2-inch cubes

- 4 ounces fresh Mexican chorizo, casings removed

- Salt

- Lime zest, finely grated

- Cilantro leaves

Directions

First, cook the chorizo in a skillet over moderate heat for 8 minutes or until lightly browned, breaking it up with a spoon.

Then scrape the chorizo into a bowl and break it into clumps.

Add 1 tablespoon of water to the skillet and simmer it over low heat.

Add butter cubes individually while whisking until each cube has melted.

Stir in the cooked chorizo and lime juice and season them with salt. Keep the mixture warm over low heat.

Meanwhile, light a grill and put the oysters on the grill, the flat side facing up.

Grill the shellfish until the shells are slightly open, then move them to a platter. Remove the top shell from the oysters using mitts or gloves.

Once done, spoon the chorizo onto the shellfish and serve it garnished with lime zest and cilantro leaf.

Serve the oysters with full-bodied wine.

38: Grilled Sea Scallops with Corn Salad

Preparation: 15 minutes

Cooking: 15 minutes

Ready-In: 30 minutes

Serves 6

Ingredients

- 1½ pounds sea scallops

- ¼ cup plus 3 tablespoons safflower oil

- 1 teaspoon Dijon mustard

- 2 tablespoons hot water

- 2 tablespoons balsamic vinegar

- 1 small shallot, minced

- Pepper, freshly ground

- Salt

- 1/3 cup basil leaves, finely shredded

- 3 scallions, light and white green parts only, thinly sliced

- 1 pint of grape tomatoes, halved

- 6 ears of corn, shucked

Directions

Boil salted water in a large pot, then cook corn for around 5 minutes or until tender.

Drain the corn and let it cool. Move the corn to a bowl and cut off the kernels.

Add basil, scallions, and tomatoes, and season with pepper and salt.

Now blend mustard, vinegar, shallots, and hot water in a blender. Then slowly add in 6 tablespoons safflower oil, the blender still running.

Once well combined, season with salt and pepper and toss it with tomatoes and corn salad.

Then, toss the remaining safflower oil with the scallops, salt, and pepper in a large bowl and set aside. Meanwhile, preheat a grill pan.

Add half of the scallops to the grill pan one at a time. Cook on medium-high heat for 4 minutes per batch or until browned, turning once.

Set the corn salad on plates and top with the grilled scallops.

39: Instant Pot Steamed Crab Legs

Prep Time: 3 minutes

Cook Time: 2 minutes

Total Time: 5 minutes

Serves: 5

Ingredients

- 2 tablespoons butter, melted

- 1 cup water

- Lemon juice

- 2 lbs. frozen crab legs

Directions

Place the steamer basket into the instant pot, then put the crab legs on it.

Add in water and lock the lid in place.

Cook for 2 minutes at high pressure, then quick-release. The crab meat, once cooked, should be bright pink.

Serve the crab legs topped with melted butter and lemon juice, then enjoy.

Section 3 v: Mixed Seafood Recipes

40: Summer Seafood Stew

Prep time: 10 Minutes

Cook time: 25 Minutes

Total time: 35 Minutes

Servings: 4-6

Ingredients

- Crusty bread or 1 cup of cannellini beans

- 1 lemon

- ½ cup of chopped flat-leaf parsley

- Salt and pepper to taste

- ½ teaspoon of chili flakes or cayenne

- 1 lb of large prawns, raw, peeled, and deveined (sub scallops)

- 1 lb of mussels (sub clams)

- 8 oz. of firm fish like halibut, tilapia, Mahi-mahi, or salmon

- 2 medium tomatoes- diced (one can of diced tomatoes and juices)

- 1 teaspoon of fish sauce (leave out if using fish stock)

- 4 cups of chicken stock (a good fish stock)

- 1 cup dry white wine

- 2 tablespoons of tomato paste

- 4 garlic cloves, smashed and roughly diced

- 1 cup of finely chopped onion (half a large onion)

- 2 cups of finely chopped fennel (one large bulb)

- 6–8 ounces of crumbled chorizo

Directions

Use a Dutch oven or a big, deep-bottom pan to cook 6 to 8 oz. of chorizo in olive oil. Remove from the casing, crumble, or split into small chunks.

As soon as it cooks, set it aside. Pour out the cooking oil, and wipe off the pan with a paper towel.

Heat 2 tablespoons of olive oil on medium-high heat in the same pan. Then add in fennel while frequently mixing for approximately 3 minutes.

Add onion, adjust heat to medium, and sauté for approximately 8 to 10 minutes or until soft.

Then add garlic, and sauté for 3 minutes, stirring now and then, until garlic becomes golden.

Add tomato paste and adjust the heat to high, stirring for approximately 3 extra minutes or until the paste darkens. You are essentially frying the paste to boost the flavor of the dish.

Add white wine and adjust the heat to medium-high, stirring for approximately 2 minutes or until halfway done.

Add fish sauce, cooked chorizo, tomatoes, and chicken stock, and bring the contents to a simmer. Then add pepper, chili flakes, and salt to flavor. If you use chorizo, the broth can be salty enough, so check to confirm.

Squeeze the chorizo with half of the lemon. Taste and adjust the flavor, then add the fish and simmer for a few minutes.

Add the prawns, simmer again for a few minutes, and then add mussels. Remember that the bigger the prawns, mussels, or fish portions, the longer they take to cook through.

NOTE: For seafood that takes the longest time to cook, add them in first.

Taste and adjust the salt and lemon to your preference.

Distribute the seafood stew among 4 to 6 bowls and top each with fresh parsley.

41: Creamy Seafood Chowder

Prep time: 10 Minutes

Cook time: 20 Minutes

Total time: 30 Minutes

Servings: 6

Ingredients

- 1 tablespoon of parsley

- 2 cups of heavy cream

- 6.5 ounces of chopped clams canned, drained

- 12 oz. of shrimp peeled and deveined

- 8 oz. of scallops

- 8 oz. white   fish cut   into   chunks (cod/salmon/tilapia/haddock)

- ½ cup of white wine

- 5 cups of broth seafood or chicken

- ½ cup of corn

- 1 pound of potatoes peeled and cubed

- 1 carrot, sliced

- 1 stalk of sliced celery

- ¼ cup of flour

- ¼ teaspoon of thyme

- 1 teaspoon of old bay seasoning

- 1 medium onion diced

- ¼ cup of butter

Directions

Cook the onion with butter until soft.

Add in thyme, vintage Bay seasoning, and flour, and cook for 2 to 3 minutes.

Add carrot, celery, potato, corn, broth, and wine & bring to a boil. Lower the heat and simmer 10 for approximately minutes.

Stir in cream and seafood. Cook the mixture for approximately 8 to 10 minutes or until the fish cooks and the potatoes are soft.

Mix in parsley and season with pepper and salt to taste.

42: Mixed Seafood Soup

Prep time: 5 Minutes

Cook time: 10 Minutes

Total time: 15 Minutes

Servings: 4

Ingredients

- 1 teaspoon of fresh coriander

- 1 teaspoon of white vinegar/rice wine vinegar

- 1 egg

- 1 tablespoon of olive oil

- 1 teaspoon of Sichuan pepper

- 1 teaspoon of Lemongrass powder

- 1 teaspoon of Kefirs lime leaf powder

- 1 teaspoon of Panda powder

- 20 grams of Spring Onion

- 10 grams of garlic

- 10 grams of ginger

- 100 ml of coconut milk

- 150 ml water

- 250 ml of fish stock

- 100 grams of prawns

- 100 grams of boneless fish fillets

- Salt to Taste

- 1 teaspoon Fish Sauce

- 1 teaspoon Soy Sauce

Directions

Begin by cutting the prawns and fish into small chunks.

Heat a tablespoon of olive oil in the wok and fry the garlic, ginger, and onion.

Add the seafood with the kefir lime leaf powder, lemongrass, panda powder, Sichuan pepper powder, salt, and stir fry.

Then mix the contents well in the fish sauce, mild soy sauce, white vinegar, and the middle part of the onion.

Add your fish stock to the water and cook for 3 to 4 minutes.

Add 1 beaten egg and mix nicely, then add the green part of the onion.

Now add in coriander and coconut milk. Once cooked through, enjoy!

43: Seafood with Lemony Soy

Preparation: 45 minutes

Cooking: 5 minutes

Ready-In: 50 minutes

Serves 16 skewers

Ingredients

- 1 pound large sea scallops

- 1 pound medium shrimp, shelled and deveined

- 2 jalapeños, very thinly sliced

- 2 lemons, very thinly sliced

- 1 cup sake

- 1 cup mirin

- 1½ cups low-sodium soy sauce

- Vegetable oil for grilling

Directions

Mix the sauce with jalapenos, lemon slices, sake, and mirin.

Then thread the shrimp in skewers, about 8 in number, then add them to the marinade. Turn to coat.

Repeat with the scallops, and keep them chilled for approximately 30 minutes. After 15 minutes, turn them through and then drain.

Then, brush the scallops and shrimp with vegetable oil and grill over high heat for around 4 minutes while turning once or twice.

Serve while hot.

44: Creamy Seafood in Garlic Wine Sauce

Prep Time: 15 minutes

Cook Time: 10 minutes

Total Time: 25 minutes

Serves: 2 or 4

Ingredients

- ½ cup heavy cream

- ¼ cup white wine

- 6 garlic cloves crushed or minced

- 2 tablespoons white onion, finely chopped

- 2 tablespoons of butter

- ½ pound bay scallops

- ½ pound calamari or squid cut into slices

- ½ pound peeled and deveined raw shrimp

- Chopped parsley

- Salt and pepper to taste

Serving ideas

- Tomato and onion curtido side salad

- Rice (Latin style)

- Fried green plantains

- Bread

Directions

Sprinkle some salt over the seafood to season it.

Heat the butter in a big skillet over medium heat until it melts.

Then add and cook garlic and onion for around two minutes.

Add the shrimp to the mixture and cook everything for about 1 minute.

Add the white wine, combine well, and cook over high heat for another 1 minute.

Add the whipping cream and heat the mixture until the prawns are almost cooked.

Then add bay scallops and the squid and cook for approximately two minutes or until the bay scallops and squid are done.

Taste and adjust the seasoning as needed.

Add the chopped parsley and combine. Serve the mixture of seafood right away with garlic sauce.

45: Seafood Stew

Prep Time: 5 minutes

Cook Time: 10 minutes

Total Time: 15 minutes

Serves: 2

Ingredients

- ⅛ teaspoon ground black pepper

- ¼ teaspoon salt

- A handful of fresh or frozen spinach

- 1 13 oz tin chopped tomatoes

- 1 teaspoon pepper flakes

- 1 tablespoon olive oil

- 3 cloves of garlic

- 1 onion

- 1 pound frozen prawns or shrimp, mussels, and squid rings

- Fresh herbs

Directions

Heat the oil in a pan.

Add the chopped onion to the cooking pan over low to medium heat and fry until golden.

Add the chili flakes and minced garlic, and then fry for one more minute.

Mix the chopped tomatoes well, and let it simmer for approximately 3-4 minutes or until the sauce thickens.

Add the frozen seafood mixture, cover, and cook over medium heat until the seafood is well cooked, or for 4-5 minutes.

Finally, add the fresh parsley or spinach, sprinkle with pepper and salt, and turn off the heat. Serve immediately!

46: Mixed Seafood in Garlic Butter Sauce

Prep Time: 15 minutes

Cook Time: 10 minutes

Total Time: 25 minutes

Ingredients

- 1 tablespoon sugar

- 1 head of garlic

- 1 block butter

- 2 corn, cut into pieces

- 500g squid

- 1 kg mussels

- 1kg shrimp

- Salt and pepper to taste

Directions

Prep the mussels by washing and debearding. Steam them in salty water until they open, drain, and set aside.

Clean and rinse the squid and then slice it. Boil the squid in the salted water for just one minute.

Boil the corn in salted water until tender. Drain, then set aside.

Melt the butter in a large wok over medium heat, then add garlic. Cook until the garlic is aromatic; add the mussels, squid, and corn and stir.

Stir in the shrimp and cook until done.

47: Mixed Seafood Grill

Serves 6

Prep 15 minutes

Cook time: 10 minutes

Total time: 25 minutes

Serves 6

Ingredients

- 1 lb deveined peeled extra-large shrimp with tails

- 1 lb. halibut, cut into 1 1/4 to 1 1/2-inch piece

- 1/4 teaspoon salt

- 1/2 teaspoon fennel seed, crushed

- 1 teaspoon lemon-pepper seasoning

- 2 tablespoons butter, melted

Directions

Heat the grill. Add the butter, fennel seed, salt, and lemon-pepper seasoning in a large mixing bowl.

Add the shrimp and halibut, toss until well coated, then put them in a grill basket.

When ready to cook, put the grill basket on a gas grill on medium-high heat or medium-high coals on a charcoal grill, about 4 to 6 inches away.

Grill the seafood for 5 to 10 minutes, or until the halibut flakes easily with a fork and the shrimp becomes pink.

48: Creamy Mixed Seafood Soup

Prep time: 20 minutes

Cook time: 20 minutes

Total time:40 minutes

Ingredients

- 2 teaspoons minced garlic

- ½ cup chopped onion

- 2 tablespoons butter

- 1 tablespoon cooking oil

- 100 grams mussels

- 100 grams white fish fillet, sliced

- 100 grams of squid, sliced into rings

- : 4 crabs, cut in half

- 10 medium size shrimps, shelled and deveined

- 2 teaspoons ginger, sliced

- 4 cups water

- ½ cup green bell pepper, cut into cubes

- ½ cup red bell pepper, cut into cubes

- 1-410 ml Angel Evaporated Filled Milk

- 1 shrimp bouillon

- 3 tablespoons all-purpose flour

- ½ cup celery, sliced

- 1 cup carrots, sliced into coins

Directions

Bring ginger and water to a boil in a big pot. Rapidly blanch the mussels, fish fillets, crabs, shrimp, and squid. Take the seafood out of the cooking pot, set it aside, but preserve the stock.

Heat the butter and oil in a separate cooking pot. Cook the garlic and onion in this cooking pot until soft and fragrant.

Add the celery and carrots and cook until the veggies cook halfway.

Mix in the all-purpose flour. Stir until mixed and heated. Add the preserved seafood stock and shrimp broth and bring to a boil.

Return the seafood to the cooking pot and add the evaporated milk. Cook for 10 to 15 minutes on low heat. Add in the red bell peppers and sprinkle them with pepper and salt.

Pour soup into serving dishes and top with freshly chopped parsley.

49: Mixed Seafood Pasta

Serves 4 people

Prep Time 30 minutes

Cook Time 5 minutes

Ingredients

- 100g trout fillet cut into chunks

- 200g prawns peeled and shells reserved

- 50 ml oil

- 100g baby spinach

- 500g linguine pasta or any pasta

- 1 handful of fresh parsley leaves to garnish

For the Sauce

- ½ glass of white wine

- 250 ml water

- 50g tomato purée

- 100 ml cream

- 1 onion, finely chopped

Directions

Start by heating a medium-sized saucepan over medium heat to prepare the sauce.

Heat the prawn shells for 3 to 4 minutes, then add the chopped onion, water, and tomato purée.

Bring the shells to a boil on low heat for about 10 minutes and strain the prawns through a fine mesh screen into a clean saucepan, discarding the shells.

Stir in the white wine and cream, then heat the mixture until reduced by one-third. Set the mixture aside.

Cook the pasta using the package directions in a stockpot of boiling salted water until al dente. Drain and keep the pasta warm.

Heat a big heavy-bottomed frying pan on medium-high. Let the cooking oil heat up to a high temperature.

Cook the peeled prawns and sea trout pieces for approximately 2 to 3 minutes. To the frying pan, add the sauce, followed by the baby spinach and pasta.

Serve the dish in a big bowl with the parsley as garnish.

Conclusion

I hope this seafood preparation book has been informative.

As you have seen, preparing seafood requires practice and enough information on handling various types of fish. I wish you the best in your seafood recipe discovery!

Finally, if you enjoyed the recipes in this book or have a question, leave a review or comment on Amazon.

I love getting feedback on the recipes. Your reviews really make a difference; thank you.

PS: I'd like your feedback. If you are happy with this book, please leave a review on Amazon.

Please leave a review for this book on Amazon by visiting the page below:

https://amzn.to/2VMR5qr